ADVENTURE TALES

A Framework for Therapeutic Story Creation by and for Children

Adapted and developed by Barr Kazer

(based on the story-telling concept of Gill Morton)

Routledge
Taylor & Francis Group

LONDON AND NEW YORK

This work has been adapted from Gill Morton's Therapeutic Story Group Model for schools which has been fully described in:

- Working with Stories in Groups (in Clinical counselling in Schools; Ed Nick Barwick, Routledge 2000).

- Using group narrative with troubled children (in *Counselling and Psychotherapy Journal*, February 2004, Vol 15 no 1).

- Therapeutic Story Groups: educational psychotherapy in a school setting (in *Why can't I help this child to learn—understanding emotional blocks to learning*, Ed Helen High, UKCP/Karnac series, Karnac books 2012).

- Safe Space for change in the outside world of school with Jill McWilliam (in *The Psychotherapist*, November 2013).

Gill Morton with Jill McWilliam and Michael Reeves (UKCP registered Educational Psychotherapists) continue to deliver their framework for embedding TSGs in schools, with associated training programmes, materials and supervision.

castlemorton@gmail.com   jillmcwilliam@metaphors.org.uk

The Caspari Foundation for Educational Psychotherapy included the Therapeutic Story Group model in their MA in Educational Psychotherapy www.caspari.org.uk.

Supplementary Resources Disclaimer

Additional resources were previously made available for this title on CD. However, as CD has become a less accessible format, all resources have been moved to a more convenient online download option.

You can find these resources available here: www.routledge.com/9781909301306

Please note: Where this title mentions the associated disc, please use the downloadable resources instead.

First published 2015 by Speechmark Publishing Ltd.

Published 2017 by Routledge
2 Park Square, Milton Park, Abingdon, Oxon OX14 4RN
711 Third Avenue, New York, NY 10017, USA

Routledge is an imprint of the Taylor & Francis Group, an informa business

Design and artwork by Moo Creative (Luton)

British Library Cataloguing in Publication Data
A catalogue record for this book is available from the British Library

ISBN: 9781909301306 (pbk)

CONTENTS

For a story truly to hold the child's attention, it must entertain him and arouse his curiosity.

But to enrich his life, it must stimulate his imagination;

Help him to develop his intellect and to clarify his emotions;

Be attuned to his anxieties and aspirations;

Give full credit to his difficulties, whilst at the same time suggesting solutions to the problems which perplex him.

(Bruno Bettelheim, 1991, p5)

ACKNOWLEDGEMENTS

This practical guide owes a huge debt of thanks to Gill Morton. Her article about group therapeutic story telling in the *Counselling and Psychotherapy Journal* (2004) was my initial inspiration for the concept of Adventure Tales. Since reading it, over the last ten years I have adapted and developed her concept of story telling in my own way and in my own workplaces. But many of the core ideas remain Gill's and I am most grateful to her on behalf of all the children with whom I have worked and helped through those ideas. Underpinning Adventure Tales are the sound therapeutic theories that Gill has meticulously researched and developed over the years. I thank her for being my inspiration.

Also with grateful thanks to:

- Lilian Beattie for dialogue

- John Hale for enriching my therapeutic practice

- Sue Edmanson for her enthusiasm and support

- Niki Lewarne for clear thinking

- Rachel Swaffield and Bridgewater School for the opportunity to develop this therapeutic journey

- the children of Bridgewater School who have given so much fun and imagination as well as sharing their pain and unhappiness

- Karla Burley and The Open Toy Box for believing in the therapeutic value of Adventure Tales

- Brian for the space to create this book.

INTRODUCTION

This framework for therapeutic story creation comprises:

- Children's Log – a printable resource, containing the core Adventure Tales framework into which the children's created Adventure Tale can be inserted quickly and easily, a chapter for each session.

- This practical guide, containing:

  - Getting started – How to run an Adventure Tales group

  - Steps for organising an Adventure Tales group

  - 'How to be' – The therapeutic process in Adventure Tales

  - Session format

  - Captain's Log

  - Children's Log – a copy of the printable version which can be photocopied

  - Glossary – some useful phrases for the recorder

  - Proformas (for photocopying): Atex outline, appointment slips, Memory Book instructions, letters for meetings, Certificate of Achievement

  - Evaluation tools (for photocopying).

Who this book is for

This Adventure Tales practical guide is to support troubled, unhappy children aged between about 7 and 12 years, children who are troubled but not in crisis. Their concerns include anything that walks through a child counsellor's door. Almost all troubled children thrive in Adventure Tales, working in a group of four children.

Adventure Tales work in metaphor, the children creating a new Adventure Tale to help them share and resolve feelings that may be unacknowledged, unbearable, suppressed or acted out. These feelings seriously undermine children's happiness and ability to function fully in their life, forming behaviours that are adverse to their well-being, eg withdrawal, aggression, sadness.

Together, four children create and illustrate an Adventure Tale about an 'Exploration into the Unknown Land'. The children are the Explorers. The counsellor and the recorder are the Captains who keep the Explorers safe and bring them safely home. The Explorers decide what actions to take or not to take in the Adventure.

The counsellor and the recorder maintain the confidentiality of any personal information given by the children. Because the work is in metaphor, the children are not revealing any 'secrets', confidentiality issues rarely arise for the children and trust is able to build rapidly within the group. Nevertheless, the children are asked to be respectful both in and outside the group of any knowledge they may have gained about each other.

At each session the Explorers are given a brief scenario by the counsellor, such as 'there is a shadow circling in the mist'. The children then offer their ideas, fears and solutions; the Captains may also offer suggestions and the chapter is created.

Each scenario thus enables children to create a unique, thought-provoking Adventure Tale which for them is exactly that – a tale or story. However, when it is read therapeutically, the Adventure Tale can be viewed as a metaphor for the children's internal journey. Unconsciously, the children bring their real-life troubles into the Adventure, disguised as monsters, dragons, deserts, volcanoes, etc – there is no end to the inventiveness of the unconscious.

Safely contained within the Adventure Tale, the children successfully overcome these adversities; they try out a new way of being; experience new, possible futures; find courage and skills within themselves; all of which transfer to real life.

The Adventure Tales group is supported by a counsellor working therapeutically with the children through the metaphors they bring to the Adventure. Each session follows the same routines, which provide consistency and the contained place where children feel safe. The routines create the creative, reflective space for the Adventure Tale making.

The recorder makes notes of the children's ideas, discussions, dilemmas and solutions thus freeing the children from worry about the mechanics of writing and releasing their creativity. Later the counsellor writes up the Adventure Tale, subtly including therapeutic insights, into the prepared, printable framework. Every session the children each receive an Adventure Tale print-out of the previous session's chapter, with their words in individual colours, and they experience the joy of reading their own words while therapeutic insights are reinforced.

The children benefit from Adventure Tales on many profound levels: therapeutically, socially and educationally. Specifically, Adventure Tales help:

- develop inter- and intra-relationships
- enhance emotional literacy
- resolve emotional issues
- improve ability to think round own problems
- improve tolerance of difference
- increase trust in other people

- stimulate the imagination

- increase self-esteem

- increase the ability to express views clearly and calmly

- increase confidence in literacy skills, especially reading.

The Adventure Tales practical guide is targeted for use in schools by a counsellor working alongside an empathic adult recorder such as a teacher, SENCo, INCo, teaching assistant or child support worker. It will also be useful to other professionals working with children in other settings. Evaluation of Adventure Tales has consistently shown that teachers and parents all observe the restorative effect of Adventure Tales as the children show a better balance of feelings and actions.

Adventure Tales groups are cost-effective: four children for ten weeks, each session costing a group counselling fee plus the cost of one hour of recorder's time.

GETTING STARTED

Each child is referred to as 'he' for consistency throughout this book. The children take on the role of Explorers, travelling on the Atex (an all terrain exploration open-topped car).

Choosing the children

Four children are chosen by a teacher who knows best the needs of the children, usually but not always a base or form teacher, a Key Stage Tutor or the SENCo or INCo. The children work best if they are from the same year group, from about Year 3 to Year 7 (7–12 years). They are chosen from:

- children in need for emotional and/or behavioural reasons (eg sad, angry, tearful, withdrawn, disruptive, traumatised)

- a mix of lively and withdrawn children

- preferably two boys with two girls to create a balance, otherwise all boys or all girls.

Experience has shown that children with Asperger's syndrome or autistic tendencies are usually best not chosen as they tend to neither benefit from nor enjoy Adventure Tales. Also unsuitable are children in crisis who will need one-to-one counselling support.

Role of the therapeutic adult – the counsellor

The counsellor is referred to as 'she' for consistency throughout this book.

An integrative method of counselling was used in developing this Adventure Tales practical guide but each counsellor will bring her own way of working. The section 'How to be' offers detailed suggestions of ways of working therapeutically that are particularly relevant to Adventure Tales and should be read alongside these notes.

The role of the counsellor in Adventure Tales is complex. She takes on the role of a Captain on the Atex. As Captain, the counsellor contains and supports the children by creating the therapeutic relationship as they travel through their Adventure on the Atex. She keeps a balance between the children in the group and ensures that each child feels heard and valued. All of this work takes place within the overarching metaphor of the Adventure Tale.

The counsellor ensures that it is the children's own Adventure, shaped by their free-ranging imagination, coloured by their fears and traumas, and resolved by their own skills and strengths. The counsellor is the trusted adult who has the responsibility to respond therapeutically and non-judgementally to all that the children bring to the group.

The counsellor also has the responsibility to sensitively offer suggestions that widen the scope of the children's thinking so that they can consider different ways of being and different consequences, hear a different viewpoint from that experienced before, and experience differing views offered in a respectful way. She widens their choices of how to behave and react.

During each session, the counsellor is herself supported by the 'Captain's Log'. This provides the Adventure Tale framework, chapter by chapter, while also offering suggestions to help the counsellor. As she becomes familiar with the Adventure Tales process, so the counsellor will develop her own ways of supporting the children in their Adventure.

At the end of each session, the counsellor facilitates a review time with the recorder, encouraging a mutual flow of observations and discussing future planning in response to the children's needs. The session notes proforma (page 65) can be used to make any notes and futures plans and to act as a memory aid. There is also an element of supervision as the counsellor keeps both the recorder and herself safe by checking out any feelings in them that might have been raised by the session. The counsellor will also be able to take any issues to her own supervisor.

After each session, the counsellor writes up the Adventure Tale as described next.

Writing the Adventure Tale

After each session, the counsellor writes the children's Adventure in the Children's Log using both the children's words as noted by the recorder and the counsellor's memories and reflections. This is the opportunity for the counsellor to subtly include insights and therapeutic moments into the Adventure (without using therapeutic jargon). The Adventure is written using words appropriate for the age group and individual reading ability.

The Children's Log contains the Adventure Tale framework identical to that in the shaded box in the Captain's Log, chapter by chapter. There is a photocopiable master version of the Children's Log on pages 43–52. There is also an identical version which can be printed out to be used and adapted as needed.

The Children's Log is designed so that each chapter of the Adventure can be inserted in the spaces provided between the framework words (in the shaded box in the Captain's Log). The **framework words** can be adjusted, enabling the counsellor to change the framework wording so that it is right for the tale of specific groups. Each finished chapter should be set in a suitable-sized font for the reading ability of the group and should be no longer than one or two A4 pages. The Adventure Tale will lose its impact if it is too lengthy when the children read each chapter out loud.

During the Adventure Tale write-up, a quick check of positive words is helpful before printing out, as actions and events often flow first when writing it up. This check will raise awareness of where more positive words and phrases are needed. They can be easily inserted. It is important for the well-being of the children, for the efficacy of the therapeutic work and for the integrity of the Adventure Tale that a similar number of positive words are used for each child.

The Adventure Tale is printed out in colours matched to the words and actions of each child (the colour each child chooses in the first session). Any small parts for the Captains are in black. Six identical colour copies of the chapter are printed and put into the Adventure Tale folders ready for the next session, one for each child, for the counsellor and for the recorder. Thus the Adventure Tales Log grows session by session.

When the chapters are received at the beginning of each session, the children will be able to instantly recognise, by colour, which parts are specific to them and to be read aloud by them. Using coloured fonts also shows the participation rates by each child in the creation of the Adventure Tale. This can be a helpful tool for the counsellor if she needs to subtly encourage more participation by quiet children or less input from a dominant child.

The role of the recorder

The recorder is referred to as 'she' for consistency throughout this book. The recorder is usually a teaching assistant, a teacher or a child support worker. She should be empathic, non-judgemental and available for all of the sessions.

She takes on the role of a second Captain on the Atex. The core role of the recorder is to make brief notes of what each child says and to note the names of speakers (the children will be quick to point out any wrongly attributed words or actions). It is helpful to the counsellor if the recorder also notes significant moments, eg anger, tears, gestures.

The recorder has an important working relationship with the counsellor. Any discussions during the sessions (eg ideas about resolving an issue in the Adventure Tale) can help the children by giving them an opportunity to experience two adults working in harmony.

The recorder is invaluable in catching and responding to any comments or actions that the counsellor misses (eg when the dialogue is too fast for one person), especially when all of the children are drawing. The recorder's task then is usually to mirror or reflect back to the child what has been said or drawn (while not forgetting to note it), so that the child feels valued. Such intervention also gives the counsellor the opportunity to respond if appropriate. The Glossary at the end of this book contains suggestions for helpful praise, mirroring and response phrases.

The post-session review with the counsellor allows time for a mutual debriefing by them and for supervision of the recorder.

Setting

The room where the sessions are held must be quiet and unlikely to be disturbed. The children need to be confident that they will not be overheard.

There should be six identical chairs and a table big enough for everyone to sit around comfortably, ideally a hexagonal shape which defines each child's space. There needs to be room on the table for the A1 drawing paper plus individual drawing space. The Captains always sit opposite each other – containing the group – the children can choose their places. Occasionally, from session to session, the children may move places, which can give valuable therapeutic knowledge.

In any school the counsellor has to accept that changes in time and venue may occasionally happen but, as long as the school has understood that consistency of routine (among many other things) is important in counselling, they are usually extremely helpful. There are a few immutable issues if the venue is changed: the new room must also be quiet and unlikely to be disturbed and the children must feel confident that they will not be overheard.

All unavoidable changes will need to be acknowledged and therapeutically dealt with in the group, so that the children feel valued: for example, if there is short notice of change; if the chairs are not identical.

Equipment needed

- *1 sheet of A1-sized strong white paper with a simple outline of the Atex drawn as viewed from above*
- *6 clip files in red, yellow, blue and green for the Adventure Tale as it grows session by session*
- *1 notepad and pen for the recorder to record the Adventure Tale*
- *4 zipped transparent folders (their Kit Bag) in red, yellow, blue and green and large enough to contain A4-sized paper. Each Kit Bag contains, in matching colours:*
  - *a pencil*
  - *no erasers (the children must learn to live with mistakes)*
  - *a pack of good quality pencil crayons*
  - *a pack of wax crayons*
  - *scissors*
  - *coloured A5-sized paper – as many different colours as possible, including brown*
  - *a glue stick*
  - *sticky tape.*
- *Whiteboard, four non-permanent marker pens and a cloth or tissues to clean it.*

STEPS FOR ORGANISING AN ADVENTURE TALES GROUP

Note: for consistency, 'parent' is used to include either or both parents, guardians or carers.

Before the Adventure Tales sessions

A certain amount of preplanning is needed before the Adventure Tales group can be started. The preplanning described below will ensure that the group runs smoothly.

1. The counsellor discusses the Adventure Tales concept with appropriate staff, including the Head, to ensure that the school gives permission and support.

2. The counsellor chooses a recorder.

3. The counsellor decides the day and the time of the sessions, which will be a weekly lesson period.

4. The room is booked for all sessions. (It can be helpful for the counsellor to plan for an extra week to allow for a missed session due to school trips, tests, etc.)

5. The appropriate teacher is asked to choose four children.

6. The teacher checks with the children that they are willing to try Adventure Tales.

7. The teacher or the counsellor speaks with each parent to explain Adventure Tales.

8. The counsellor contacts each parent (by phone is most effective) to arrange separate pre-Adventure Tales meetings, each meeting to include parent, child and counsellor. They are an opportunity for parents to discuss Adventure Tales and meet the counsellor. Confirmation letters of the date and time are sent out (see page 59).

9. The room is booked for the parent meetings.

10. The counsellor gives out the children's appointment slips (see page 57) on the day of the meeting by whichever method suits the school, eg by hand to the appropriate teacher or in registers. Or the children can be given their own appointment slips for the next session at the end of each session.

11. At the pre-Adventure Tales meeting, each parent is asked to complete, with the child, the 'Reasons for concern' evaluation form (see page 68–9). Before finishing the meeting, the counsellor books the post-Adventure Tales meeting with the parent.

12. The teacher or the counsellor explains to the staff which lessons will be missed during Adventure Tales and discusses how the children will catch up with work.

13. The counsellor meets the appropriate teachers to discuss the children and asks the teachers to fill in their pre-Adventure Tales 'Reasons for concern' evaluation form (see page 68) with the help of the 'Concerns Guide for Teachers (see page 66).

14. The counsellor prepares the equipment for the first Adventure Tales session.

During the Adventure Tales sessions

This section gives the administrative details. The session format section (page 15) explains in depth how each session is run.

1. The counsellor gives out the children's appointment slips on the day of Adventure Tales, either by hand to the teachers or in the registers.

2. The sessions are run.

3. After the penultimate session, the counsellor prepares the equipment for the final session.

After the Adventure Tales sessions

After the children have had their final session, there are various tasks to complete to ensure a safe ending for the group.

1. The counsellor checks by phone with the parents, a week before the due date, that they can still attend their post-Adventure Tales meetings.

2. The room is booked for the parent meetings.

3. Before the meetings the counsellor copies the initial concerns from the pre Adventure Tales Reasons for Concern form onto the 'post Adventure Tales Reasons for concern' form (see page 69). At the meetings, each parent and child is asked to re-scale these original concerns on the post Adventure form. This second meeting will only include the child at the beginning of the meeting, to help the rescaling of concerns. The child then returns to class. To be sure the child does not feel excluded or pushed out, the counsellor can say something such as she knows the child has read all the Tale and now it is the turn of the parent. This is because the meeting may involve some interpretation of the Adventure to relate it to real-life issues. The Adventure works best for the child if all of the Tale is left in the metaphor. For parent meeting session notes, see page 64. Possible ways forward for the child can be discussed. For feedback notes, see page 71.

4. For the teachers, the counsellor copies their initial concerns from the pre Adventure Tales Reasons for Concern form onto the 'post Adventure Tales Reasons for concern' evaluation form (see page 69). She asks the teachers to re-scale these original concerns on the post Adventure form. Possible ways forward for the child can be discussed. For feedback notes, see page 71.

5. The counsellor prepares two 'Concerns Scaling Score sheets' (p 70), one using the teachers pre and post scores and the other using parent scores. These are given to the Head and appropriate teachers.

'HOW TO BE' – THE THERAPEUTIC PROCESS IN ADVENTURE TALES

Notes for the counsellor

These notes provide the therapeutic input that is particularly relevant to Adventure Tales. Each group will be different; each counsellor will have a different approach. These notes are intended as guidance for the counsellor as she works with these diversities.

Creating a strong therapeutic relationship with the children

Within a strong therapeutic relationship, the children can benefit from the many therapeutic experiences associated with counselling. Creating and working within a strong therapeutic relationship, including within groups, has been explored many times by many very able, thoughtful therapists. It is recommended that they are read extensively by the counsellor as they will greatly enhance the Adventure Tales experience for the children. The theory behind Adventure Tales is comprehensively and sensitively explored by Gill Morton (see the Bibliography).

Within the therapeutic relationship

The counsellor:

Stays in the Adventure. The Adventure Tale is the metaphor by which children can bear to look at their concerns because *they are one step away*.

The resolving of the concern in the metaphor helps the child cope better with the concerns of real life that had given rise to the metaphor.

Responds as she would in real life to the children's concerns in the Tale, eg if in the Tale they are angry, lonely. She therapeutically helps the child deal with those feelings, emotions and scenarios as she would in real life *but* always helping through the Tale events and characters, staying in the metaphor.

Does not ask 'why' they have created an idea or reacted in certain ways because this will break the Adventure Tale thread. If the counsellor comes out of the Adventure Tale, eg by asking 'Why did you think that?', the child loses contact with the inner mind, is thrown back to the often unbearable reality, and the restorative effect is lost.

Thinks deeply about 'why' and uses this knowledge to shape her later therapeutic comments.

Encourages the use of very detailed, clear descriptions to help the children imagine as much as possible about an object or a creature or an action. This focuses their brain and fixes it in their mind; if they choose to draw the image, it is then further established. Any therapeutic work involving this image is therefore enhanced. For example, if the children see a bottle in the water, the counsellor encourages them to see clearly: what it is made from, size, colour, decorations, top, handles, fastenings, etc.

Ways to be on the Adventure

The counsellor:

Acknowledges and encourages the children's ideas. She accepts them non-judgementally so that the children feel valued and listened-to.

Is proactive. Once the children have given their ideas, she respectfully offers new ways of finding solutions, widens their choices of response, shows new ideas of what is possible, stretches their imaginations, offers a picture of alternative, possible futures and ways of being.

Stimulates thinking about consequences, making them explicit, before the children make their final decisions. She shows they are responsible for the consequences of their choices. Learning this skill can help protect impulsive or risk-taking children; it can enable children to take responsibility for their actions.

Sets safety boundaries and is prepared to veto an action if a suggested action would put a child in danger. For example, if a child wants to go alone and unprotected into a jungle, the counsellor discusses ideas for a 'safety net' that could make the action safe, so that the child experiences being protected and being cared for. They are also being shown how to look after themselves, which is important for a child who may not be protected at home.

Listens to and accepts non-judgementally all safe decisions or choices that the children make in the Adventure Tale. This allows them to feel in control of this part of their lives; lives which often have left them powerless. Also, in the secure place of the group, children can learn from any mistaken choices.

Praises, praises, praises for every genuine achievement in behaviour, however small; and for things some children find very hard, eg if they made a choice, or managed to wait. The children will feel valued, raising their self-esteem.

Acknowledges the smallest signs of hidden, masked feelings or emotions such as flickers of fear or anger, so that the children experience being listened to, heard, valued, cherished and looked after. These tiny signs are often the indicator of huge, hidden emotions, so that acknowledging the tiny signs actually touches the child very deeply and they may become more open to sharing and to therapeutic change.

- If the counsellor gets the wrong emotion, the child will ignore her comment! No harm is done.

- If the counsellor is right, how wonderful! The child will feel understood and recognised, and be more likely to share more of themselves.

- Once 'it' is explicit yet held safely, 'it' becomes more bearable and thus more open to the possibility of change or acceptance.

Offers respect for all and expects respect for all. Disrespect is a form of bullying. The counsellor:

- makes explicit group interactions such as ignored or endured comments, snide asides and irritable glances

- comments explicitly when respect does not happen and catches the smallest hint

- asks the others to show how they are affected by the disrespect

- is aware that sometimes respect was there but was misunderstood by the victim because of their private logic, their own perception of life

- allows space and time for working in the group therapeutically both with the child who gave offence and with those who were affected by it.

Containment in a safe place

All is contained in the metaphor so that the children look, reflect and resolve troubles at one remove, then experience the restorative effect in real life.

The Atex, the Adventure Tale framework and the routines consistently and safely hold the creative, reflective, therapeutic space where the Adventure Tale is experienced.

The Adventure provides a space for the child to be free:

- from their mistaken goals and their private logic

- from past baggage and perceptions

- to be the child; to move towards their own developing adult.

The children:

Are not alone. They have two adult helpers to contain their emotions, to keep them safe while they experience dangerous events or feelings; they have a safe base – the Atex; they have companions who offer support or new ways forward.

Can 'play' and so look at things differently, and experiment with new skills.

Can try out their true self without fear of mistakes, reprisals or ridicule. This enables children to experience and develop good social ways of being in both inter- and intra-relationships.

Are safe to show their dark side (eg anger, hate, revenge) because:

- their dark side is acknowledged

- they are given boundaries of safe containment where they are shown explicitly that some responses are unacceptable

- they learn that they are not all dark or all light, that we are all a mixture of both.

Learn that it is *what we do with the dark side* that matters, finding new ways to be, instead of old habits of response or reaction. For example, anger channelled safely can be a great energiser for change.

Feel safe to admit fears through the metaphor, as the fear is one step removed from reality and they trust that they will receive help to ensure their safe survival.

'Light bulb' moments need to be acknowledged at that time by the counsellor if a child realises the parallels with real life (eg as in 'My mum behaves like that'), but if possible she doesn't follow it up. Continuing with the Adventure shows that while she has recognised the child's distress, she is also showing that his fear or concern need not be overwhelming; it is possible that it can be contained. She trusts the Adventure Tale.

However, if his distress is severe, the counsellor suggests to the child that they talk afterwards, then she continues the Adventure. At the end of the session, she has that talk. If it is not practical immediately, she arranges a meeting time as soon as possible.

Occasionally, the troubles will all spill out regardless and the counsellor has to accept this. One of the two adults may need to move away with the child in order to listen and to talk with him. It may have to be dealt with then and there as a Child Protection issue, following the school's policies.

The rest of the group should continue the session, the remaining Captain helping them to find an acceptable way of including the distress of the child into the Adventure Tale while leaving the group feeling safe and contained.

SESSION FORMAT

Session length

Each session lasts for a lesson time, which may vary according to the age of the children, but an hour works well. The Adventure Tale lasts for 50 minutes, followed by 10 minutes of 'wind down' time. This is a valuable time in which the children build relationships and 'play'. A whiteboard for writing and drawing on is very popular.

For these last 10 minutes the Captains will clear up and then, if possible, have a separate space in which to start privately reviewing the session. Ideally, they will use a small side room that is near to the children, to ensure that discipline is maintained, so that the children continue to feel safe. Otherwise, the children may need to return to their classes for the last 5–10 minutes.

In a busy school day it is often difficult to continue the review session for the 20–30 minutes that will be needed. Planning the time of the session immediately before a school break could help to solve this difficulty because, usually, the recorder is so enthused by Adventure Tales that she will forgo her free time. If either Captain has to leave for another lesson, they agree a meeting time later that day or as soon as possible. See the session notes on page 65.

Later, the counsellor writes up and prints out six colour copies of the Adventure Tale.

The Adventure Tale Scenarios

The Adventure Tale Scenarios form the basis of the Captain's Log, which creates a 'therapeutic map' of the Exploration. The Captain's Log is written in chapters, one chapter per session. In each chapter the Adventure Tale Scenario is printed in the shaded box. These words in the shaded box are spoken by the counsellor during each session.

The scenarios are chosen to enable the children to experience and respond to a wide range of emotional situations. For example, the Storm sequence often resonates with children who have experienced a sudden family break-up, illness or death.

The same Adventure Tale Scenarios are also in the Children's Log, forming the basis of the children's Adventure Tale as it is written up by the counsellor.

Guidance

In the Captain's Log, anything not printed in the shaded box is only for the counsellor (the Captain). The questions and comments are a guide and support for the counsellor. They are written as briefly as possible to facilitate quick reference during the sessions. For this reason they are written in the imperative. They can be reworded according to what most helps the children and what most fits the counsellor's personal style. Other comments and questions can be added.

The first two chapters offer detailed guidance to give the counsellor support as she finds her own way of being with the children in the Adventure Tale. The last chapter of the Captain's Log also contains detailed guidance. All of the intermediate chapters continue to offer some support.

As the counsellor becomes familiar with the Adventure Tale process, after giving the scenario, she can adjust what happens according to the needs of each group. For example, with younger children or children with special needs, acting their ideas through drama can be an effective, practical way of stimulating problem solving.

The Routines

The Routines are the same for each session. They give consistency throughout the sessions, enhancing the secure framework. The Routines help to contain and support the creative, reflective and therapeutic Adventure Tale space of the sessions. The Routines may be changed from group to group, but they need to stay consistent for any one group. The following Routines have been shown by experience to support the group well.

Preparation Routine

Before the children arrive the counsellor places on the table the A1 sheet of paper with the Atex outline covered. (It is kept covered at first because otherwise it distracts the children's attention from the Routines.) She also puts out the children's Kit Bags, the Adventure Tale folders and the recorder's notepad and pen.

Beginning Routine

The counsellor greets everyone. The previous session's chapter is read aloud, each child reading their colour, and the recorder reading any normal black type.

Adventure Tale Scenario Routine

The counsellor uncovers the Atex and outlines the scenario for the chapter, using the words printed in the shaded box. Then the vital core of the Adventure Tale begins. The Explorers create, talk about and experience the new adventure, the counsellor works therapeutically within the Adventure Tale metaphor and the recorder supports this work while taking notes.

The counsellor may need to comment that it is OK to be silent. Paradoxically, a silent child then often talks, as if relaxing or as if being given permission to speak. The children usually quickly notice that not talking means there is not much of their colour in the Adventure Tale write-up; they respond by joining in more next session. If not, the link between speaking and coloured Adventure Tale words can be gently shown and talking encouraged.

Discussion Routine

This may or may not be needed, depending on the dynamics of the group.

The counsellor explains the method of response she expects from the children, choosing what suits the group best in any one session. Different methods suit different groups and different stages in the process. For example, the children may:

- answer as they are ready, or
- put up their hands, the first being chosen, then the second, and so on, or
- take turns round the table, eg if one child is very dominant or reticent, or
- choose to 'pass'.

Planning and Action Routine

The counsellor acknowledges all of the different ideas the children give and offers more if needed to widen their thinking. She may discuss group cooperation versus individual tasks.

She acknowledges that there are different comfort levels of risk taking for each of us while, as appropriate, stretching the comfort zones of timid children. If a child is a risk-taker and wants to go alone in the Adventure Tale action, the counsellor discusses ways to keep them safe. Or she puts boundaries in place by saying 'No, that is not allowed as you would not be safe'.

Differing ideas are resolved by discussion and by taking the majority view. If necessary, a vote can be taken.

Resolution Routine

The counsellor ensures there is a resolution of the situation if at all possible and that it is made explicit in the children's final plan of action. If there is no resolution in one session, this needs to be acknowledged and the theme revisited and resolved in the next session. Rarely, the counsellor may need to acknowledge that sometimes we just don't know the answer, that it is hard living with the unknown or with things that have to be accepted.

Once resolution is achieved, and the children have chosen their final action plan, the recorder checks that she has recorded it correctly.

Because of time constraints, the Captains and the Explorers will usually have to presume, once the planning is finished, that the action has actually taken place.

Drawing Routine (allow at least 15 minutes)

The recorder continues taking notes during this time.

The children choose to draw anything they want from the scenario. The children choose paper for drawing on from their Kit Bags. There are no erasers as everyone has to accept their mistakes and make the best of them that they can. If they wish, they may colour their drawings. The drawings are cut out and placed by the Explorers wherever they wish on the sheet of A1 paper. Then they must wait before sticking down the drawings because each Explorer must respect the others by checking with all the other Explorers whether that position is OK. If not, negotiations are needed so that mutual respect is experienced. This is why no one may draw directly on the A1 paper. Only when all agree can they stick anything down on the A1 paper.

Ending Routine

The counsellor says it is time to leave the Atex. All agree the next meeting time and place. The Explorers pack their Kit Bags. If possible, the Explorers have ten minutes' 'wind-down' in the room before their next lesson.

CAPTAIN'S LOG

INTRODUCTION

In the Captain's Log, the text printed in the shaded box is said aloud in the group. Anything else, not printed in the shaded box, is only for the counsellor (the Captain). The questions and comments are a guide for the counsellor. They are written as briefly as possible to facilitate quick reference during the sessions. For this reason they are written in the imperative. They can be used or reworded, according to what most helps the children and what most fits the counsellor's personal style. Other comments and questions can be added.

The first two chapters offer detailed comments to give the counsellor support as she finds her own way of being with the children in the Adventure Tale. The final chapter of the Captain's Log also contains detailed guidance. All of the intermediate chapters continue to offer some support.

MEETING THE ATEX

Preparation Routine

Start the session by carrying out the routine on page 16 and then follow the procedure described below.

Introduction

Introduce yourself and the recorder with your proper names.

Practicalities

Explain to the children:

- Where to meet.
- The length of a session – which may have to link with the length of school lessons – ideally, 50 minutes for the Adventure Tale and 10 minutes' wind-down. Younger children may need a shorter time.
- The sessions are weekly for a term.
- They will need to catch up on missed lessons.
- There will be about 10 sessions.
- As much notice as possible will be given if there are changes in time or place.
- They will have an appointment slip on the day.

Explaining the Exploration

It will be a journey on the Atex, an all terrain exploration open-topped car, into the Unknown Land. What happens on the journey will create the Adventure Tale. It will be the children's Adventure Tale, created from their ideas and imagination. The children will not need to write down anything, that is the task of the recorder, but they will be drawing some pictures.

You and the recorder are the Captains for the journey; the children are the Explorers.

Choosing the colours

Each child chooses the colour – red, yellow, blue or green – that they will be for the Exploration; this will be the colour of their Adventure Tale Kit Bag and their Adventure Tale folder. Most importantly, this is the colour typed in the Adventure Tale to match each child's words. To show how valued each child is, they learn that each of them has an equal right to a colour.

Routledge Taylor & Francis Group

21

CHAPTER 1

They choose in a way that keeps their choice private until they all show their chosen colour at the same time. One way is for each child to put a crayon pack under the table, take out their chosen colour crayon, then show them all at the same time. If two or more choose the same colour, resolving this dilemma is part of the Adventure Tale process.

Each child then receives their colour Kit Bag.

Chapter 1 Meeting the Atex. The Adventure Tale begins.

Adventure Tale Scenario Routine

> *The Atex is waiting at the roadside. It is ready to go exploring on a journey, an Exploration into the Unknown Land – and back again. There are four Explorers and two Captains. They meet at the roadside and introduce themselves.*

Names on the Atex

Everyone chooses their new name for when they are on the Atex:

- Captain … and Captain …

- Explorers choose their own names.

Characters

Each Explorer chooses who or what they want to be on the Exploration:

- look like anything they want

- boy, girl or creature, big or small, long or short hair, special costume or not, any colour skin.

Captains' Promise

- Avoid a straight promise to keep them safe, as unexpected things do happen in real life.

> *As Captains, we promise to do our utmost to keep the Explorers safe and bring you back again. Also, the Atex is completely safe: it cannot break down, overturn or sink. Nothing can come on the Atex unless the Explorers choose to let it do so.*

Routledge
Taylor & Francis Group

Rules

First, go through the Discussion Routine (page 17) if needed.

The Rules on the Atex are chosen by the Explorers.

• Rephrase the Explorers' words to clarify, if necessary.

• Stimulate ideas, eg by thinking of school behaviour expectations.

• Ensure core values are included, eg respect for each other, acceptance of different view points.

> *Here are the Rules of the Atex as decided by the Explorers ...*

Drawing Routine

See page 18.

• The Explorers draw themselves as the Being they have chosen to look like.

• Both Captains draw themselves – this is the only time you will draw.

• Start a discussion about baggage while the Explorers are drawing themselves.

> *The Explorers take on board two pieces of baggage and a picture if they wish.*

This can be:

• something special they don't want to leave behind

and/or

• something they might want on the Adventure.

Drawing Routine

See page 18.

• The Explorers will choose where to put the Captains on the Atex.

• They put all of the drawings on the Atex.

> *The Atex is ready to start. It is time for the Explorers and Captains to go on board with their baggage. They travel off into the Unknown Land.*

Ending Routine

See page 18.

 Ɍ Routledge Taylor & Francis Group

CHAPTER 2

THE BOTTLE

Preparation Routine

See page 16.

Beginning Routine

See page 16.

Adventure Tale Scenario Routine

> Chapter 2 The Bottle. The Atex is travelling along when, suddenly, a Bottle is seen floating down a river.

- Ask the Explorers each to describe what they can see.
- Remember to encourage very detailed descriptions.
- Encourage details of size, colour, what the Bottle is made from, any tops or fastenings.
- Accept that each child sees a different Bottle.

> *The Explorers guess what might be inside the Bottle.*
>
> *Together, the Explorers make a decision about bringing it to the Atex.*

The choices are:

- yes
- no, but acknowledge that not knowing can be difficult
- if no, then try to encourage yes. If definitely no then move on to the Chapter 3 scenario.

> *They decide whether they want the Bottle on board the Atex – there is a risk, it might be dangerous.*

- Consider whether the risk level is acceptable.
- If not, consider alternative places to keep the Bottle, eg in a trailer behind the Atex.

> *Next, the Explorers all work out how the Bottle can be brought safely to the Atex.*
>
> *Plans and Action!*

R Routledge Taylor & Francis Group

Planning and Action Routine

See page 17.

Discussion Routine

If this is needed, see page 17.

Resolution Routine

See page 17.

> **Finally, the Explorers have to choose to open the Bottle – or not.**

- Discuss the risk.
- Often, they need to suspend belief and accept there will be different contents for each child even though there is only one Bottle.

> **What do they find?**

- Remember to use detailed descriptions!
- Is any action needed for the safe storage of contents?

Drawing Routine

See page 18.

> **Darkness falls and they all rest quietly after their brave efforts with the Bottle.**

Ending Routine

See page 18.

THE MISTY HOLLOW

Preparation Routine

See page 16.

Beginning Routine

See page 16.

Adventure Tale Scenario Routine

> Chapter 3 The Misty Hollow. The Atex is travelling calmly across a meadow. Suddenly, the Explorers find themselves riding down into a mist-filled Hollow. They cannot see clearly but there is a shadow circling around them in the mist. They try to see what it is.

- Acknowledge all of their ideas.

> *The Shadow cannot get on the Atex but it may make them lose their way. The Explorers all decide what to do about the Shadow. They can choose to ...*

- Acknowledge the children's ideas, then suggest any of the following if they missed them:

  ❖ pretend it isn't there
  ❖ frighten it away
  ❖ kill it
  ❖ catch it
  ❖ befriend it.

> *Plans and Action!*

Planning and Action Routine

See page 17.

- Praise, praise, praise.
- Check – the Explorers choose roles for each child suitable for their therapeutic needs.
- Use detailed descriptions about methods – specify tools, equipment and action.

R Routledge
Taylor & Francis Group

Resolution Routine

See page 17.

Drawing Routine

See page 18.

Now that the Explorers have brilliantly succeeded in sorting out what to do about the Shadow, everyone can sleep safely on the Atex while it travels on through the night in the clear air.

Ending Routine

See page 18.

CHAPTER 3

R Routledge Taylor & Francis Group

27

THE STORM

Preparation Routine

See page 16.

Beginning Routine

See page 16.

Adventure Tale Scenario Routine

> Chapter 4 The Storm. The clouds have gone dark and have thickened, the wind is rising, and a storm is coming. The rain begins, the wind gets louder and louder. The River nearby rises higher and higher until the Atex is afloat. It rocks and sways.

> *The Explorers have to think quickly what to do. They know the Atex cannot sink but they are getting very uncomfortable, cold and wet.*
>
> *Plans and Action!*

Planning and Action Routine

- Praise, praise, praise.

- Maybe a cover is needed for the Atex.

- How to pass the time while sheltering.

- Encourage the use of detailed descriptions for important actions, inventions and ideas.

Resolution Routine

See page 17.

 Ⓡ Routledge
Taylor & Francis Group

Drawing Routine

See page 18.

> *The Storm has blown away. The wind has dropped. The rain has stopped.*
> *The water in the River goes down and the Atex is on dry land again.*
> *The Explorers have weathered the Storm; all are safe and sound. What*
> *amazing skills the Explorers have shown!*

- Make explicit their roles achieved and skills used.

> *The Explorers now rest quietly, enjoying the peace after the Storm.*

Ending Routine

See page 18.

CROSSING THE RIVER

Preparation Routine

See page 16.

Beginning Routine

See page 16.

Adventure Tale Scenario Routine

> Chapter 5 Crossing the River. Now that all is calm, the Explorers can see an Island in the River. What can they see on the Island?

- Are there trees, mountains, volcanoes, monsters, food, sun, rain, etc?

> **The Explorers choose whether or not to cross the River to the Island.**

- You hope that they say yes! If not, go to a nearby island and create a scenario where they have to land, eg run out of fresh water.

> **The Captain lands on a sheltered beach. The Atex will be completely safe. On the Beach the Explorers can see ...**

- Explain that the Beach will be a safe and pleasing place.

> **The Explorers make Camp using lots of different ideas about how to build shelters.**

- Encourage the use of imagination, local and natural stuff, maybe with a little help from the Atex stores.
- Create tents, tree houses, caves, burrows, etc.
- Make beds or hammocks.

R Routledge
Taylor & Francis Group

> **The Explorers sort out:**
> - **finding things to eat and drink**
> - **who will cook it and how to cook it.**

- Check that the roles for the children are suited to their therapeutic needs.

> **Night has fallen by the time the Explorers have finished setting up Camp. It is time to settle down to rest.**

Ending Routine

See page 18.

Note: if the school term is short, Chapter 6 can be combined with Chapter 7 in one session.

EXPLORING

Preparation Routine

See page 16.

Beginning Routine

See page 16.

Adventure Tale Scenario Routine

> Chapter 6 Exploring. In the morning light, the Explorers can see the Ruins of a castle on the Island. There seems to be something moving in the Ruins. It's time to explore! To keep themselves safe, the Explorers take with them:
> * food and drink
> * special clothes
> * special equipment

> *The Explorers follow a path leading from the Camp. The Path goes through ...*

* Offer a choice: eg boulders, grass, swamp, jungle, volcanoes, desert.

> *As the Explorers go along the Path, they hear something ahead. They wonder about it and, maybe, feel fear – could it be a monster or an ambush? They discover it is:*

* Remember to use detailed descriptions.

> *The Explorers discuss what they should do next.*
> *Plans and Action!*

 Ｒ Routledge
Taylor & Francis Group

Planning and Action Routine

See page 17.

Resolution Routine

See page 17.

Drawing Routine

See page 18.

> *The Explorers have done well; all are safely past the thing on the Path. They should be proud of their skills and strengths and of overcoming their fears.*

- Praise, praise, praise: the fears overcome, eg for each child, according to their therapeutic needs.

Ending Routine

See page 18.

Ɍ Routledge
Taylor & Francis Group

THE CELLAR IN THE RUINS

Preparation Routine

See page 16.

Beginning Routine

See page 16.

Adventure Tale Scenario Routine

Chapter 7 The Cellar in the Ruins. After the adventures on the Path, finally the Explorers have reached the Ruins. They find a Cellar in the Ruins. They can see very little because it is dark inside. Maybe it's a bit scary. There is a risk. It is good to be careful.

- Explore the dark side, our fears.
- Show that it is OK to be scared.

The Explorers think about what they need to be brave and ready enough to go inside the Cellar and explore.

- Discuss accepting help.
- Recap their abilities and strengths:
  - skills
  - help
  - special equipment.

Now the Explorers feel ready to explore. However, in the front of the Cellar they can see ...

- Accept that what is 'seen' may be different for each child.

Ɍ Routledge
Taylor & Francis Group

> *The Explorers discuss how they are going to get past, so that they can get into the Cellar.*
>
> *Plans and Action!*

Planning and Action Routine

See page 17.

Drawing Routine

See page 18.

Resolution Routine

See page 17.

> *At last, after another successful adventure, the Explorers want to go inside the Cellar. But night is falling, so they wisely decide to wait for the morning light.*

Routledge
Taylor & Francis Group

THE RESCUE

Preparation Routine

See page 16.

Beginning Routine

See page 16.

Adventure Tale Scenario Routine

> Chapter 8 The Rescue. Hiding at the back of the Cellar there is something or someone.

> *As their eyes get used to the darkness, the Explorers can see that the Being is a prisoner. They decide to rescue it. First, they find out how it is being kept prisoner.*
>
> *The Explorers choose how to rescue the Being while staying safe.*
>
> *Plans and Action!*

Planning and Action Routine

See page 17.

Resolution Routine

See page 17.

Drawing Routine

See page 18.

> *Wow, that was amazing and so courageous! Just think of all the strengths and skills the Explorers used and how their fears were overcome.*

R Routledge
Taylor & Francis Group

- Praise, praise, praise.

- Be specific for each child, according to their therapeutic needs.

> *The Explorers decide what to do with the Being, what is best for themselves and best for the Being.*

- Discuss the consequences and responsibilities.

> *Next, the Explorers decide whether there is anything in the Cellar which they would like to take with them to Camp or the Atex.*

- If their choices are very materialistic, widen their thinking

> *The Explorers go safely back to the Camp after their long day. Tomorrow will be their last day on the Island before returning home on the Atex. Endings can be sad. But first, before leaving, there will be a celebration of their fantastic success and bravery.*

Ending Routine

See page 18.

Routledge
Taylor & Francis Group

CELEBRATION TIME!

Preparation Routine

See page 16.

Beginning Routine

See page 16.

Adventure Tale Scenario Routine

> Chapter 9 Celebration Time! Today the Explorers celebrate all of the wonderful things they have done in their adventures.

- Encourage memories of special therapeutic significance for each child, of deeds, inventions, people met, treasures found.

> **Plans and Action!**

Planning and Action Routine

See page 17.

> **The Explorers choose how to celebrate.**

- Encourage all to offer ideas, possibly linking with children's resolution moments.

- Who will come to the Fun Time:

- What they will do: (swimming, games, dancing, lazing around)

- What they will wear:

- Who will bring food: (anything yummy and safe to eat and drink – this is a party)

- What kind of music they will have:

Routledge Taylor & Francis Group

> **Have a great Fun Time!**

Drawing Routine

See page 18.

- Encourage the Explorers to talk about endings and the feelings that endings may raise.

NB. It is mportant that each child draws themselves in party clothes to put on Atex.

> *Night is falling. The Atex is now ready to leave. It is time to say goodbye and leave the Island. When the Explorers wake in the morning, they will be back home at the roadside.*
>
> *They may feel a bit strange and have mixed feelings – sad, empty, lonely, as well as maybe happy, excited to be home. The Explorers will have all the memories of their amazing adventures even though the Exploration is ended.*
>
> *Go Safely, Live Well!*

Ending Routine

See page18.

FINAL SESSION

Tasks before the final session

- Complete each Adventure Tale folder by writing up and printing out the final chapter.

- Make six A4 sized colour copies of the finished A1 Atex with the children's drawings and put one at the front of each Adventure Tale folder.

- Write personal, positive comments on sticky notes from yourself and from the recorder for each child and each other, using your therapeutic knowledge. It is helpful to have slightly bigger notes than the Explorers use, to allow more space for your comments.

- Have ready small sticky notepads in a variety of colours to give the children a choice.

- Make 'Memory Books' (page 58) in a variety of colours to give the children a choice.

- Make four Certificates of Achievement (page 61) signed by yourself, showing that each child has successfully completed the Atex Exploration.

ENDINGS

Preparation Routine

See page 16 and include the following:

- Put out the Memory Books and the small sticky notepads.

Beginning Routine

- Remind the children of the need to respect each other's roles in the Adventure Tale even after they leave the group.

- Explain to the children that there is only time to read the final chapter in the session. They will have to wait for their own time to re-read all of the Adventure Tale. The Explorers and Captains each choose a 'Memory Book' to title and date.

- The Explorers each choose a sticky notepad.

- Give out your prepared sticky notes.

- The Explorers think about something good and positive that they have learned about each other. They then write and sign these positive, very brief comments on sticky notes.

- The Explorers give their sticky notes to each other (and to themselves if they choose) to be put in their own Memory Books.

Ⓡ Routledge
Taylor & Francis Group

- If they wish, the Explorers share with the group the comments they have received.

- The Memory Books can be decorated if there is time.

- Make a formal presentation of Certificates, acknowledging the importance of their achievements.

The children will each take home:

- an Adventure Tale folder
- a Memory Book
- a Certificate.

The final goodbyes are said.

Go Safely, Live Well!

CHILDREN'S LOG

CHAPTER 1
MEETING THE ATEX

The Atex is waiting at the roadside. It is ready to go exploring on a journey, an Exploration into the Unknown Land – and back again. There are four Explorers and two Captains. They meet at the roadside and introduce themselves.

As Captains, we promise to do our utmost to keep the Explorers safe and bring you back again. Also, the Atex is completely safe: it cannot break down, overturn or sink. Nothing can come on the Atex unless the Explorers choose to let it do so.

Here are the Rules of the Atex as decided by the Explorers:

The Explorers take on board two pieces of baggage and a picture if they wish.

The Atex is ready to start. It is time for the Explorers and Captains to go on board with their baggage. They travel off into the Unknown Land.

R Routledge
Taylor & Francis Group

CHAPTER 2
THE BOTTLE

The Atex is travelling along when, suddenly, a Bottle is seen floating down a river.

The Explorers guess what might be inside it.

Together, the Explorers make a decision about bringing the Bottle to the Atex.

They decide whether they want the Bottle on board the Atex – there is a risk, it might be dangerous.

Next, the Explorers all work out how the Bottle can be brought safely to the Atex.

Plans and Action!

Finally, the Explorers have to choose to open the Bottle – or not.

What do they find?

Darkness falls and they all rest quietly after their brave efforts with the Bottle.

Routledge Taylor & Francis Group

CHAPTER 3
THE MISTY HOLLOW

The Atex is travelling calmly across a meadow. Suddenly, the Explorers find themselves riding down into a mist-filled Hollow. They cannot see clearly but there is a shadow circling around them in the mist. They try to see what it is.

The Shadow cannot get on the Atex but it may make them lose their way. The Explorers all decide what to do about the Shadow. They can choose to:

Plans and Action!

Now that the Explorers have brilliantly succeeded in sorting out what to do about the Shadow, everyone can sleep safely on the Atex while it travels on through the night in the clear air.

R Routledge Taylor & Francis Group

CHAPTER 4
THE STORM

The clouds have gone dark and have thickened, the wind is rising, and a storm is coming. The rain begins, the wind gets louder and louder. The River nearby rises higher and higher until the Atex is afloat. It rocks and sways.

The Explorers have to think quickly what to do. They know the Atex cannot sink but they are getting very uncomfortable, cold and wet.

Plans and Action!

The Storm has blown away. The wind has dropped. The rain has stopped. The water in the River goes down and the Atex is on dry land again. The Explorers have weathered the storm; all are safe and sound. What amazing skills the Explorers have shown!

The Explorers now rest quietly, enjoying the peace after the Storm.

R Routledge
Taylor & Francis Group

CHAPTER 5
CROSSING THE RIVER

Now that all is calm, the Explorers can see an Island in the River. What can they see on the Island?

The Explorers choose whether or not to cross to the Island.

The Captain lands on a sheltered beach. The Atex will be completely safe.

On the Beach the Explorers can see:

The Explorers make Camp using lots of different ideas about how to build shelters.

The Explorers sort out:

- finding things to eat and drink

- who will cook it and how to cook it.

Night has fallen by the time the Explorers have finished setting up Camp. It is time to settle down to rest.

CHAPTER 6
EXPLORING

In the morning light, the Explorers can see the Ruins of a castle on the Island. There seems to be something moving in the Ruins. It's time to explore! To keep themselves safe, the Explorers take with them:

- food and drink

- special clothes

- special equipment.

The Explorers follow a path leading from the Camp. The Path goes through:

As the Explorers go along the Path, they hear something ahead. They wonder about it and, maybe, feel fear – could it be a monster or an ambush? They discover it is:

The Explorers discuss what they should do next.

Plans and Action!

The Explorers have done well, all are safely past the thing on the Path. They should be proud of their skills and strengths and of overcoming their fears.

Routledge
Taylor & Francis Group

CHAPTER 7
THE CELLAR IN THE RUINS

After the adventures on the Path, finally the Explorers have reached the Ruins. They find a Cellar in the Ruins. They can see very little because it is dark inside. Maybe it's a bit scary. There is a risk. It is good to be careful.

The Explorers think about what they need to be brave and ready enough to go inside the Cellar and explore.

Now the Explorers feel ready to explore. However, in the front of the Cellar they can see:

The Explorers discuss how they are going to get past, so that they can get into the Cellar.

Plans and Action!

At last, after another successful adventure, the Explorers want to go inside the Cellar. But night is falling, so they wisely decide to wait for the morning light.

 R Routledge
Taylor & Francis Group

CHAPTER 8
THE RESCUE

Hiding at the back of the Cellar there is something or someone.

As their eyes get used to the darkness, the Explorers can see that the Being is a prisoner. They decide to rescue it. First, they find out how it is being kept prisoner.

The Explorers choose how to rescue the Being while staying safe.

Plans and Action!

Wow, that was amazing and so courageous! Just think of all the strengths and skills the Explorers used and how their fears were overcome.

The Explorers decide what to do with the Being, what is best for themselves and best for the Being.

Next, the Explorers decide whether there is anything in the Cellar which they would like to take with them to Camp or the Atex.

The Explorers go safely back to the Camp after their long day. Tomorrow will be their last day on the Island before returning home on the Atex. Endings can be sad. But first, before leaving, there will be a celebration of their fantastic success and bravery.

Routledge
Taylor & Francis Group

CHAPTER 9
CELEBRATION TIME!

Today the Explorers celebrate all of the wonderful things they have done in their adventures.

Plans and Action!

The Explorers choose how to celebrate.

- Who will come to the Fun Time:

- What they will do: (swimming, games, dancing, lazing around)

- Who will bring food: (anything yummy and safe to eat and drink – this is a party)

- What they will wear:

- What kind of music they will have:

Have a great Fun Time!

Night is falling. The Atex is now ready to leave. It is time to say goodbye and leave the Island. When the Explorers wake in the morning, they will be back home at the roadside.

They may feel a bit strange and with mixed feelings – sad, empty, lonely, as well as maybe happy, excited to be home. The Explorers will have all the memories of their amazing adventures even though the Exploration is ended.

Go Safely, Live Well

GLOSSARY

Some ways of encouraging a child to have further thoughts

✓ And more? … and more? … and more?

✓ Do you think …?

✓ Five fingers are shown and ticked off as ideas are suggested, giving the expectation of more and more.

✓ I wonder if you tried/did … what do you think might happen?

✓ …. might be a good idea.

✓ That's a great idea! How many more can you suggest?

✓ That's fine.

✓ That's OK.

✓ What else could you do?

✓ … which is fine/OK

Suggestions for positive words and phrases

The following words and phrases can be used both during the session and in the write-up. Positive words, when used in a genuine way, really do help to lift a child's self-esteem. It can take a minimum of six positive phrases to offset one negative comment. Many children come to Adventure Tales with a back history of receiving negative comments, even from birth. In order to flourish, children need positive feedback.

Paradoxically, children who are unused to praise may struggle to accept it. Therefore, to hold the trust of a child, it is vital that the praise is true to the child's character and action. Otherwise there is a strong risk of breaking trust between the adult and child, with the child either ignoring the comment or maybe thinking 'I knew I couldn't believe them, they are just like everyone else'.

The following list of positive words and phrases includes various parts of speech. Many are adjectives, which can be changed to adverbs, usually by adding 'ly'. The list is arranged into groups of words and phrases with similar meanings.

Ɽ Routledge
Taylor & Francis Group

Useful words

brave	creative	calm	accomplish	confused
brilliant	imaginative	clear	achieve	fearful
clever	inventive	helpful	celebrate	nervous
congratulations	practical	neat	lead	scared
courageous	responsible	polite	overcome (something)	uncertain
delicious	useful	quiet	succeed	worried
excellent	•	thoughtful	success	
great	discovers	willing	survive	
magnificent	fixes		well-earned	
marvellous	offers			
special	volunteers			
wise				
wonderful				
wow				

Useful phrases

bursting with ideas	be aware of risk
does well to	be careful
good team member	be cautious
good leader	keep in touch
high five	keep themselves safe
plans well	look after themselves
prepares well	wise not to rush in
work well together as a team	•
worked very hard to…	achieved
•	at last
after a lot of discussion	finally
after much debate	found a solution
after much effort/thought	solve by …
difficult discussion	which is fine
hard to decide	which is OK
spent a lot of time and energy	
split two ways … take a vote	
takes time … eventually	
used their skills	
waited patiently	

Ⓡ Routledge
Taylor & Francis Group

DIAGRAM OF THE ATEX

Routledge
Taylor & Francis Group

APPOINTMENT SLIPS

Appointment slip

Dear_____ Form: _____ Year: _____

You have Adventure Tales today_____ at Lesson _____

when we shall be pleased to see you in the _____

Appointment slip

Dear_____ Form: _____ Year: _____

You have Adventure Tales today_____ at Lesson _____

when we shall be pleased to see you in the _____

Appointment slip

Dear_____ Form: _____ Year: _____

You have Adventure Tales today_____ at Lesson _____

when we shall be pleased to see you in the _____

Appointment slip

Dear_____ Form: _____ Year: _____

You have Adventure Tales today_____ at Lesson _____

when we shall be pleased to see you in the _____

Appointment slip

Dear_____ Form: _____ Year: _____

You have Adventure Tales today_____ at Lesson _____

when we shall be pleased to see you in the _____

Routledge Taylor & Francis Group

MEMORY BOOK

Create about eight to ten books as follows in A4-sized different coloured papers (including red, yellow, blue and green) to give the children a choice of colour. Crease all folds sharply.

Fold the paper along the fold 1 line (see diagram below). Keeping the fold at the top, fold along fold 2 and then fold 3 so that the edges overlap. Cut out triangles 1 and 2 of the overlap to create a fastening.

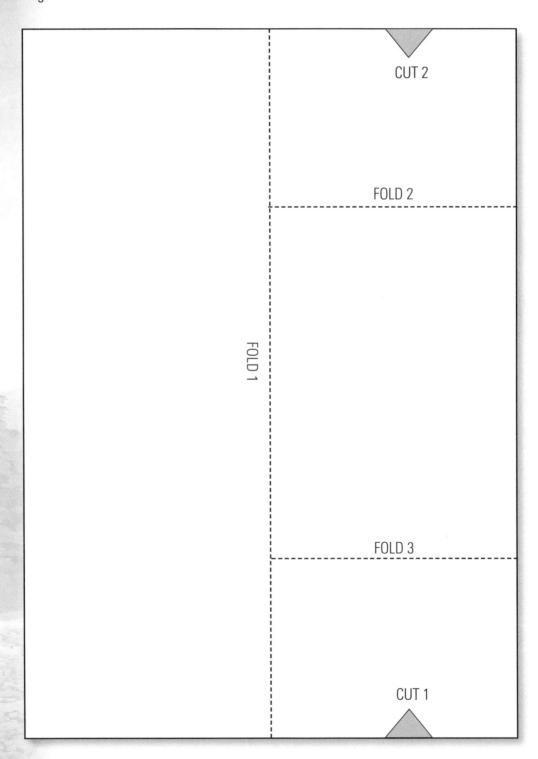

Routledge
Taylor & Francis Group

LETTERS FOR MEETINGS

Confirmation of parent meeting

Dear

I am writing to introduce myself. I am one of the School Counsellors at
_____ and my name is _____.

This term I am taking a small group of children for Adventure Tales and I am able
to offer a place to _____.

Adventure Tales involves speaking, listening and writing activities and is
intended to develop self-esteem, empathy, creativity and communication
skills. Each session lasts for one lesson period with myself and a teaching
assistant, _____. They will take place on a _____ day, for 10 weeks
starting _____.

In my experience Adventure Tales works best for the child when it is clear that
home, school and child are all working together. Therefore, before your child starts
the Adventure Tales group, I should welcome a meeting of about 30 minutes with
_____ and you at school. This will give you an opportunity to talk to
me and to find out more about Adventure Tales before your child starts the group.

I confirm that we shall meet at _____ on _____.

I look forward to meeting you and _____.

Yours sincerely

LETTERS FOR MEETINGS

Confirmation of final parent meeting

Dear

The Adventure Tales sessions end soon. Your child _____ will be bringing home the amazing Adventure written about their 'Exploration'.

It would be good to meet with you for about 30 minutes to look at the finished Adventure Tale and to think about any differences it has made to your child that you may have noticed.

I confirm we will be meeting at _____ on _____.

With best wishes

Routledge Taylor & Francis Group

CERTIFICATE OF ACHIEVEMENT

Congratulations

_____

YOU HAVE SUCCESSFULLY COMPLETED

THE ADVENTURE

Signed

_____

Date

Routledge
Taylor & Francis Group

EVALUATION TOOLS

PRIVATE AND CONFIDENTIAL
ADVENTURE TALES THERAPEUTIC GROUP PARENT MEETING SESSION NOTES

Group start date	Group end date

School

Date	Parent/s	Child	Date	Parent/s
Session 1			Session 2	

Date	Parent/s	Child	Date	Parent/s
Session 1			Session 2	

Date	Parent/s	Child	Date	Parent/s
Session 1			Session 2	

Date	Parent/s	Child	Date	Parent/s
Session 1			Session 2	

Counsellor

ADVENTURE TALES THERAPEUTIC GROUP SESSION NOTES

School	Start date	End date

Parent permission received: Yes /No/Not required   Evaluation completed: Start/End

Additional monitoring completed: Start/End (Type used SDQ/YP CORE/Other (specify) _____)

Focus of Session 1 Date	**Focus of Session 6** Date
Focus of Session 2 Date	**Focus of Session 7** Date
Focus of Session 3 Date	**Focus of Session 8** Date
Focus of Session 4 Date	**Focus of Session 9** Date
Focus of Session 5 Date	**Focus of Session 10** Date

Routledge
Taylor & Francis Group

ADVENTURE TALES - CONCERNS GUIDE FOR TEACHERS

Group start date	Group end date

Choose your three concerns from the following and grade them on the scales provided.

10 = Extreme concern level

5 = Reasonable/moderate concern level

0 = No concern level

1. Anger/aggression, verbal

    a. towards peers

    b. towards adults

2. Anger/aggression, physical

    a. towards peers

    b. towards adults

3. Self-harm

4. Sad/tearful

5. Depressed

6. Anxious

7. Withdrawn/self-isolates

8. Bullying

    a. Bullies others

    b. Has experienced or does experience bullying from others

9. Frequent absence

    a. irregular patterns

    b. regular patterns

10. Daydreams

11. Distracts others in class (describe)

12. Shouts out

13. Wanders in class

14. Uncooperative

15. Other

When describing these on the evaluation sheet, please provide as much detail as you wish, including how long this has been an issue.

Any action/strategies suggested or agreed in relation to the issues identified

1.

2.

3.

Is there anything else you would like to add?

Review date:

PRE-ADVENTURE TALES - REASONS FOR CONCERN

Child's name:		School:
Year group & age	Gender: Male/Female	Date: End
Number of sessions since last evaluation		Completed by Your name

Please identify up to 3 main behaviours or concerns you have about this child
(include any impact for you, them or others)

1.

| | |

Please grade the severity of this issue (0 = no concern; 5 = reasonable concern; 10 = extreme concern)

0	1	2	3	4	5	6	7	8	9	10

2.

| | |

Please grade the severity of this issue (0 = no concern; 5 = reasonable concern; 10 = extreme concern)

0	1	2	3	4	5	6	7	8	9	10

3.

| | |

Please grade the severity of this issue (0 = no concern; 5 = reasonable concern; 10 = extreme concern)

0	1	2	3	4	5	6	7	8	9	10

POST-ADVENTURE TALES - REASONS FOR CONCERN

Child's name:		School:	
Year group & age	Gender: Male/Female	Date:	End
Number of sessions since last evaluation		Completed by	Your name

Please scale again your concerns that you had about this child

(include any impact for you, them or others)

1.

Please grade the severity of this issue (0 = no concern; 5 = reasonable concern; 10 = extreme concern)

0	1	2	3	4	5	6	7	8	9	10

2.

Please grade the severity of this issue (0 = no concern; 5 = reasonable concern; 10 = extreme concern)

0	1	2	3	4	5	6	7	8	9	10

3.

Please grade the severity of this issue (0 = no concern; 5 = reasonable concern; 10 = extreme concern)

0	1	2	3	4	5	6	7	8	9	10

CONFIDENTIAL

ADVENTURE TALES - CONCERNS SCALING SCORE SHEET

Child's name		School	
Year group and age		Gender	
Concerned person (teacher or parent)		Counsellor	

Score						
10						
9						
8						
7						
6						
5						
4						
3						
2						
1						
0						
	Pre-AT Concern 1	Post-AT Concern 1	Pre-AT Concern 2	Post-AT Concern 2	Pre-AT Concern 3	Post-AT Concern 3

 Routledge Taylor & Francis Group

FEEDBACK ADVENTURE TALES GROUP

What difference have you noticed at home?
What difference has the child talked about in his/her life?
Any difference noticed in school by staff:
Any changes noticed during story telling by counsellor:
1. Any action/strategies on concern 1
2. Any action/strategies on concern 2
3. Any action/strategies on concern 3
Is there anything else you would like to add?
Review date:

Counsellor:	Adult:

Routledge
Taylor & Francis Group

BIBLIOGRAPHY

Bettelheim B (1991) *The Uses of Enchantment*, first published 1976, London, Penguin Psychology.

Morton G (2000) 'Working with stories in groups', Barwick N (ed), *Clinical Counselling in Schools*, London, Routledge.

Morton G (2004) 'Using group narrative with troubled children', *Counselling and Psychotherapy Journal*, February, 15 (01), pp21–23.

Morton G (2012) 'Therapeutic story groups: educational psychotherapy in a school setting', High H (ed), *Why Can't I Help This Child to Learn?*, London, Karnac Books.

See also:

Attwood T (1998) *Asperger's Syndrome*, London, Jessica Kingsley.

Beattie FCL (2005) *The Elemental Wheel: from Metaphor to Meaning*, London, Adlerian Society Year Book, pp125–48.

Bowlby J (1965) *Child Care and the Growth of Love*, 2nd edn, London, Penguin Original.

Casement P (1985) *On Learning from the Patient*, London, Routledge.

Edwards B (1999) *The New Drawing on the Right Side of the Brain*, London, Harper Collins.

Elliot M (1998) *Bullying*, Wise Guides, London, Hodder.

Geldart K & Geldart D (2001) *Working with Children in Groups*, Basingstoke, Palgrave.

Holmes J (1993) *John Bowlby & Attachment Theory*, London, Routledge.

Lawley J, Sullivan W & Tompkins P (2005) 'Tangled spaghetti in my head – clean language', *Therapy Today*, 16 (8), pp32–36. (Further information is available at Cleanlanguage.co.uk)

Malchiodi CA (1998) *Understanding Children's Drawings*, London, Jessica Kingsley.

Miller A (1997) *The Drama of Being a Child*, London, Virago.

Mills JC (1999) *Reconnecting to the Magic of Life*, Hawaii, Imaginal Press.

Mills JC & Crowley RJ (1986) *Therapeutic Metaphors for Children and the Child Within*, London, Routledge.

Owen N (2001) *The Magic of Metaphor*, Carmarthen, Crown House Publishing.

Pennebaker JW (2011) *The Secret Life of Pronouns – What Our Words Say about Us*, London, Bloomsbury Press.

Pratchett T (2007) *Wintersmith*, London, Corgi.

Sunderland M (2003) *Helping Children with Feelings*, A Guidebook series, Milton Keynes, Speechmark Publishing.

Van der Kolk BA (2005) 'The neurobiology of childhood trauma and abuse', Talk at the Centre for Child Mental Health. See also in *Child and Adolescent Psychiatric Clinics of North America* (2003), 12 (2), pp293–317, ix.

West J (1996) *Child Centred Play Therapy*, 2nd edn, London, Arnold.

Routledge Taylor & Francis Group

Wilkinson MA (2005) 'The Mind–Brain Relationship', London, CCYP conference. See also her papers in the *Journal of Analytical Psychology*.

Wilson J (2003) *Child-focused Practice*, London, Karnac.

Winnicott DW (1971) *Playing and Reality*, London, Tavistock/Routledge.

Winnicott DW (1980) *The Piggle*, London, Penguin.

Worley P (2012) *The if Odyssey*, London, Bloomsbury.

T - #0006 - 270721 - C0 - 297/210/4 - SB - 9781909301306 - Gloss Lamination